HOW TO SURVIVE IN
THE ARCTIC AND ANTARCTICA

LOUISE SPILSBURY

PowerKiDS press.

New York

Published in 2013 by The Rosen Publishing Group, Inc.
29 East 21st Street, New York, NY 10010

Produced for Rosen by Calcium Creative Ltd
Editors for Calcium Creative Ltd: Sarah Eason and Jennifer Sanderson
US Editor: Sara Antill
Designer: Simon Borrough

Photo credits: Cover: Shutterstock: Pyshnyy Maxim V, Sergey Tarasenko Jacheslavovich. Inside: Dreamstime: Steve Allen 7r, 17cl, Logray 16c, James Steidl 19c; Library of Congress 6c; National Science Foundation: Glenn Grant 10c, 22c, Patricia Hofmeester 13t, Chad Naughton 23c, Peter Rejeck 28cl, Derek Rogers 24cl, Mark Sabbatini 11c; Shutterstock: ALPO 18c, Andrew Buckin 14l, 26l, Pablo H Caridad 25t, Erwin F 8cl, Fivepointsix 29c, Volodymyr Goinyk 4l, 10l, 16l, 22l, 27c, 28l, Fred Hendriks 6l, 18l, Aron Ingi 8l, 20l, Karina Kononenko 12c, Nik Niklz 21t, Marteric 9t, PhotoHappiness 4tr, Armin Rose 12l, 24l, Uryadnikov Sergey 14c, Wild Arctic Pictures 4c, 20c, Jan Martin Will 15c, Gary Yim 26cr.

Library of Congress Cataloging-in-Publication Data

Spilsbury, Louise.
How to survive in the Arctic and Antarctica / by Louise Spilsbury.
    p. cm. — (Tough guides)
Includes index.
ISBN 978-1-4488-7866-6 (library binding) — ISBN 978-1-4488-7931-1 (pbk.) — ISBN 978-1-4488-7937-3 (6-pack)
1. Wilderness survival—Polar regions—Juvenile literature. I. Title.
GV200.5.S64 2013
613.69—dc23

2011051883

Manufactured in the United States of America

CPSIA Compliance Information: Batch #SW12PK: For Further Information contact Rosen Publishing, New York, New York at 1-800-237-9932

CONTENTS

SURVIVAL!

The Arctic and the Antarctic Circle are the world's coldest places. Here, the water is frozen into snow and ice. This makes it so dry that these places are called cold deserts.

The Arctic is a huge frozen ocean. It is covered in ice that is very thick in some places. In summer the edges of the ocean melt, but in winter it is frozen over.

Arctic

ARCTIC
WHERE: the region of the world around the **North Pole**
TEMPERATURE: can drop below -67° F (-55° C) in winter

I SURVIVED

In 1911 Douglas Mawson and two other scientists left their Antarctic base to do scientific research. One of the men, along with their tent, their sled, some of the dogs that pulled the sled, and most of the supplies, fell into a hole in the ice and were lost. To stay alive, the other two men ate the sled dogs. Only Mawson finally made it back to base.

Antarctica is Earth's fifth largest **continent**. It is so cold that no one lives there. The scientists who stay in **research bases** in Antarctica mostly come in summer.

Antarctica

ANTARCTIC CIRCLE
WHERE: the region of the world around the **South Pole**, including Antarctica and the surrounding ocean
TEMPERATURE: can drop below -100° F (-73° C) in winter

KEEPING WARM

One of the biggest challenges in places with icy temperatures day and night is keeping warm. In the past **inuit** people wore clothes made from **caribou** and other animal skin. The fur helps to trap a layer of warm air next to the skin. They also wore boots made from waterproof seal skin.

Inuit people

THE PARKA
WHAT: a hooded coat
FACT: Inuit people invented the parka, which is worn today by people visiting the poles

In Antarctica, icy winds that blow at 200 miles per hour (322 km/h) can freeze your skin in seconds. Wear a hood, gloves, hat, and scarf, and pull drawstrings tight so cold air cannot get in. Wear several thin, warm layers but avoid thick clothes that might make you sweat, because sweat can freeze on your body.

hat and hood

TOUGH TIP

Watch out for **frostbite**. You will notice a white patch of frozen skin on someone's face before they do. If they start mumbling and stumbling, they may be getting **hypothermia**, so you will need to get them warm, fast!

WARM CLOTHES
PROBLEM: the face and head lose heat easily and quickly
ACTION: cover head and face. Pull parka hood tight to keep out cold.

SNOW SHELTERS

No one can survive dangerously cold temperatures for long without shelter. Scientists who come to study at the poles bring materials to make buildings because there are few trees there to supply wood. They often build bases on legs to keep floors off icy ground. It also stops snow from piling up in front of doors and trapping them!

research shelter

RESEARCH SHELTER
PROBLEM: scientists need to study in remote places
ACTION: research shelters contain everything needed to stay alive in the icy temperatures of the poles

igloo

Inuit people once built snow shelters called igloos. You can build one if you are stranded outdoors. Use a saw to cut hard snow into thick, rectangular blocks. Make a circle for a base with some blocks and then put more on top, leaning them in toward the top to make a **dome**.

TOUGH TIP

Dig an underground tunnel for an entrance and block it with a rucksack to keep in the heat and keep out the wind. Never sleep directly on the ground. Lay down on top of bags or clothes so your body does not freeze.

IGLOO
SIZE: most igloos are big enough for one family
HOW: each block of snow is about 4 feet (120 cm) long, 2 feet (60 cm) wide, and 8 inches (20 cm) thick

FINDING FOOD

When it is very cold you need to eat more. This is because your body is using energy to try to keep you warm. It is too cold for many plants to grow at the poles, so most visitors bring their own food or catch it from the sea.

emperor penguin

EMPEROR PENGUIN
SIZE: grows up to 50 inches (127 cm) long and weighs 100 pounds (45 kg)
FOOD: people have had to eat penguins to survive

In the Arctic, polar bears are too difficult and dangerous to hunt, so instead people catch seabirds, seals, and fish. You can smash or cut holes in the ice and catch fish on a fishing line.

making a hole in the ice

ICE FISHING
SIZE: most ice-fishing holes are 8 inches (20 cm) wide
THREAT: if you smash the ice it may crack back to where you are standing

MELTING WATER

At the Arctic and Antarctic there is no freshwater. Freezing temperatures keep water frozen into stretches of white ice and snow that people cannot drink. To make drinking water, you need to melt ice and snow.

drinking melted snow and ice

DRINKING WATER

PROBLEM: Arctic and Antarctic air is very dry and it makes you thirsty

ACTION: drink at least 24 cups (5.6 l) of water every day

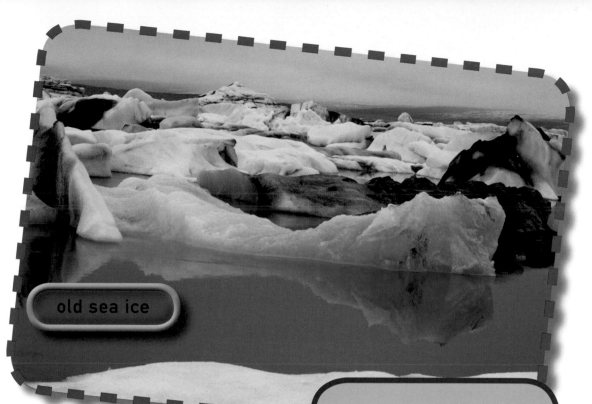

old sea ice

Arctic ice forms from seawater. New ice is gray, hard, and so salty you cannot drink it even if you melt it. As ice gets older, the salt drains out of it. Look for old sea ice that is bluish and breaks easily so that you can melt and drink it.

TOUGH TIP

Do not melt snow in your mouth to get water. This can make your body even colder and increase the risk of hypothermia. The difference in temperature between your stomach and the freezing snow can also cause painful cramps.

SEA ICE
NEW SEA ICE: gray-white, thin, full of bubbles that contain salt
OLD SEA ICE: blue, thick, fewer bubbles, less salt

ANIMAL ATTACKS

Keep a look out for the polar bear, the largest and deadliest **predator** in the Arctic. Its powerful legs, sharp teeth, and massive claws make it very dangerous. Its white fur **camouflages** it against the snow so it can sneak up on **prey**. It can swim fast enough to catch a seal in the water and on land it can outrun a person!

polar bear and cub

POLAR BEAR
SIZE: grows up to 8.2 feet (2.5 m) long
THREAT: powerful arms and sharp claws can kill in an instant

14

The leopard seal is named for its black spotted coat. Like the leopard, this Antarctic predator is big, powerful, fast, and fierce. It uses its mighty jaws and long teeth to kill smaller seals, fish, and squid. Leopard seals have sometimes attacked humans.

leopard seal

LEOPARD SEAL
SIZE: grows up to 12 feet (3.5 m) long
THREAT: strong jaws and long teeth can injure and even kill

ENDLESS SUN

In the summer months the Sun never sets at the poles. It shines all day, every day. You may feel cold but you are at risk of severe sunburn here because **ultraviolet rays**, or UV rays, reflect off snow onto skin. It is vital to cover up and wear strong sunblock on lips, ears, chin, and even under your nose.

polar sunshine

STRONG SUN

WHAT: snow reflects 90 percent of the sunlight that falls on it

THREAT: UV rays in sunlight cause redness and blisters and can burn off skin

16

Sunglasses are just as important here as they are on a sunny beach. Sunlight shining off snow can damage eyes so badly that it can cause **snow blindness**. That is when your eyes get sunburned and you cannot see well.

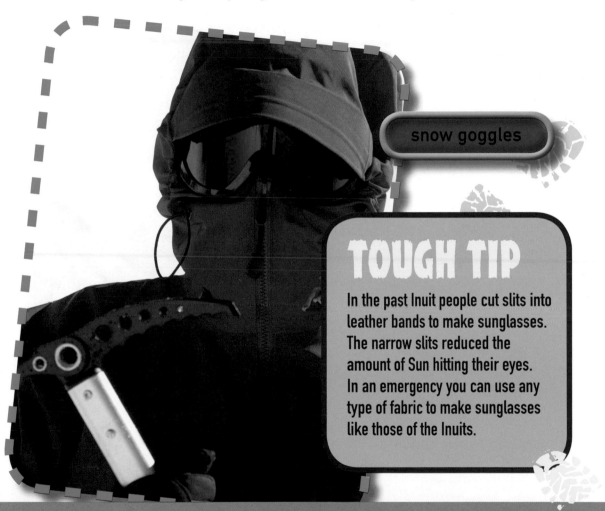

snow goggles

TOUGH TIP

In the past Inuit people cut slits into leather bands to make sunglasses. The narrow slits reduced the amount of Sun hitting their eyes. In an emergency you can use any type of fabric to make sunglasses like those of the Inuits.

SNOW GOGGLES
PROBLEM: reflected sunlight at the poles can cause snow blindness
ACTION: snow goggles stop UV rays and protect eyes

GETTING AROUND

One of the best ways to get around on snow and ice is on a motorized sled called a **snowmobile**. It has tracks like a tank to stop it from sinking into snow and to help it grip slippery ice. It has handlebars that turn skis at the front to steer and help you glide over the snow at high speed.

snowmobile

SNOWMOBILE
SPEED: up to 100 miles per hour (160 km/h)
HOW IT WORKS: engine runs on fuel

In the past Inuit people made **kayaks** from **driftwood** or animal bone and covered them in seal skin. They used packs of dogs to pull their sleds. Sled dogs have thick coats to keep warm and wide, flat feet to grip the snow.

snow shoes

TOUGH TIP

Make yourself a pair of snow shoes. Bend a stick into a loop. Tie sticks across it like a tennis racket and tie it onto your foot. Snow shoes spread your weight over a wider area so you do not sink so deep into the snow.

SNOW SHOES
WHAT: invented by Inuit people. Made of wood with leather laces.
HOW THEY WORK: wide, flat surface stops feet from sinking into the snow. Today snow shoes are usually made of plastic or metal.

FINDING YOUR WAY

Everywhere looks much the same in a snowy landscape, so how do you find your way? In the past, Inuit people used the position of the Sun, Moon, and stars in the sky to **navigate**. Watching wildlife can help, too. Most seabirds fly toward the sea during the day and return at night.

gulls

GULLS
WHAT: seabird with long bill and wide webbed feet. Often white with black markings on head or wings.
WHERE: one species in Antarctica and nine in the Arctic

Today most snowmobiles are fitted with a **Global Positioning System**, or GPS. These electronic gadgets send and receive signals from **satellites** circling high above Earth. They can be used to find where you are and to guide you to where you want to go.

I SURVIVED

On his 1914 expedition across the Antarctic, Ernest Shackleton's ship sank and the crew was stranded. Shackleton and five others went to find help in a small boat. They succeeded thanks to the navigating skills of Frank Worsley, who used a **sextant** to find their location.

GPS DEVICE
WHAT: a system that communicates with satellites in the sky
HOW: links up with four or five satellites to find a location

BLIZZARD!

A blizzard is a snowstorm in which violent, freezing winds toss snow around in the air. A blizzard is dangerous because when snow whirls around, it becomes impossible to find your way even a few feet between tents, huts, or vehicles. You can get lost in seconds.

blizzard

SEVERE BLIZZARD
WIND SPEED: can be anywhere between 35 and 100 miles per hour (72—160 km/h)
VISIBILITY: zero

One solution is to string "blizz lines" between buildings. These are ropes that people hold when they walk between buildings. If a blizzard strikes they can follow the rope to safety.

It is vital to watch the weather at all times. When a storm begins, get to a shelter quickly.

I SURVIVED

Keizo Funatsu was dog sledding across Antarctica when a blizzard hit and he was separated from the rest of his team. He dug a trench in the snow and jumped out every 30 minutes to do exercises to keep warm. After a long, terrifying night alone, his teammates found him in the morning.

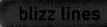
blizz lines

BLIZZ LINES
WHAT: short for "blizzard lines"
HOW THEY WORK: strong, thick ropes between buildings keep you from getting lost and blowing away

23

CRACKS AND CREVASSES

One of the biggest dangers at the poles is something you cannot see until it is too late. **Crevasses** are deep cracks in an **ice sheet** that walkers can fall into. These cracks may be only inches (cm) wide at the surface, but they can be 100 feet (30 m) or more deep!

crevasse

CREVASSE

WHAT: ice moves slowly, all the time. This can make it split apart to form crevasses.

THREAT: falling into a deep crevasse can kill a person

snow bridge

The problem is that these cracks are often covered by a frozen bridge of snow. If a snow bridge breaks as you walk over it, you may find yourself tumbling into the icy depths of a hidden crevasse, or even into the ocean.

TOUGH TIP

Crevasses covered in snow are very hard to spot until it is too late. Most teams of people tie themselves together with a long, very strong rope. Then if one person falls, the others can pull him or her back out before he or she reaches the bottom.

SNOW BRIDGE
WHAT: buildup of snow across a gap. Can be just inches (cm) thick.
THREAT: if you walk across one and it breaks, you may fall into a crevasse

ICEBERG!

If you are arriving at the poles by ship you need to watch out for icebergs. Icebergs are enormous pieces of ice that float in the sea. They form when chunks of ice break off suddenly from an ice sheet and crash into the water. Icebergs are as hard as rock and can make a hole in the side of any ship that runs into them.

iceberg

ICEBERG
SIZE: from 3 feet (1 m) high and 16 feet (5 m) long to 240 feet (74 m) high and 670 feet (204 m) long
THREAT: 90 percent of an iceberg is hidden underwater

I SURVIVED

In 1912 many people believed the *Titanic* was unsinkable because of its new safety features. When it struck an iceberg that was mostly hidden underwater, it sank overnight. There were not enough **life boats** for all of the 2,224 passengers, so more than 1,500 people died.

Smaller icebergs are difficult to see before it is too late. Big icebergs are a danger, too, because the part you can see above water is only the tip of the iceberg. The part of an iceberg hidden from view below the water is much, much bigger.

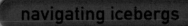

navigating icebergs

ICEBERG SAFETY
THREAT: icebergs can sink ships
ACTION: crew watches for icebergs

BE PREPARED

The Arctic and Antarctica are among the toughest places on Earth. Today more and more people travel to the North and South Poles to see these wildernesses for themselves. Visitors to the area should be prepared for anything, in case the worst happens and they find themselves stranded in the snow!

tourist boat

TOURISTS

NUMBER: more than 37,000 people visited Antarctica between 2009 and 2010

PROBLEM: most came in boats that would sink if they hit an iceberg

No one sets out from a base without a pack of supplies, even if they are out only on a day trip. You should always try to take food, water, spare clothes, sleeping bags, radios, cooking stoves, tents, and other supplies with you. At the poles, only the tough can survive!

I SURVIVED

In 2007 a ship full of tourists sank after hitting an iceberg. Its 154 passengers had only minutes to escape into life boats. Luckily a rescue ship was nearby so they had to wait for just five hours in icy temperatures, but it could have been far worse!

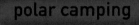

polar camping

EMERGENCY TENT
THREAT: to survive at the poles you must stay dry and warm
ACTION: carry a lightweight, strong, windproof, and waterproof tent. It should be fire resistant so you can cook inside it.

GLOSSARY

camouflages (KA-muh-flahj-ez) When an animal's skin or fur matches its surroundings.

caribou (KER-eh-boo) A reindeer.

continent (KON-tuh-nent) One of the seven large landmasses on Earth.

crevasses (krih-VAS-ez) Deep, open cracks in glaciers.

dome (DOHM) A type of curved roof.

driftwood (DRIFT-wuhd) Wood washed ashore by the sea.

expedition (ek-spuh-DIH-shun) A major trip to an area that is not well known.

frostbite (FROST-byt) When part of the body is damaged by cold.

Global Positioning System (GLOH-bul puh-ZIH-shun-ing SIS-tum) A device that helps find your location on a map.

hypothermia (hy-puh-THUR-mee-uh) When the body's temperature is too low.

ice sheet (EYES SHEET) An area of ice that covers a large area of land.

Inuit (IH-new-it) A group of people who live in northern Canada, parts of Alaska, and Greenland.

kayaks (KY-aks) Boats similar to a canoe.

life boats (LYF BOHTZ) Boats that people escape into when their ship sinks.

navigate (NA-vuh-gayt) To find one's way around.

North Pole (NORTH POHL) The northernmost point on Earth.

predator (PREH-duh-ter) An animal that hunts and eats other animals.

prey (PRAY) An animal that is hunted and eaten by other animals.

research bases (REE-serch BAYS-es) Buildings where scientists work and study.

satellites (SA-tih-lyts) Electronic devices high in space that move around Earth.

sextant (SEKS-tant) A tool for measuring angles and distances.

snow blindness (SNOH BLYND-nes) Temporary blindness caused by light reflecting off snow.

snowmobile (SNOH-moh-beel) A vehicle that can move over snow and ice.

South Pole (SOWTH POHL) The southernmost point on Earth.

ultraviolet rays (ul-truh-VY-uh-let RAYZ) Rays from the Sun that burn skin.

FURTHER READING

Clarke, Penny. *Scary Creatures of the Arctic*. Danbury, CT: Children's
     Press, 2008.

Doak, Robin. *Arctic Peoples*. First Nations of North America. Chicago:
     Heinemann–Raintree, 2011.

Ipellie, Alootook. *The Inuit Thought of It: Amazing Arctic Innovations*.
     Toronto, ON: Annick Press, 2007.

Latta, Sara. *Ice Scientist: Careers in the Frozen Arctic.* Wild Science Careers.
     New York: Enslow Publishers, 2009.

Morris, Neil. *Living in the Arctic.* World Cultures. Chicago:
     Heinemann–Raintree, 2007.

WEBSITES

Due to the changing nature of Internet links, PowerKids Press has
developed an online list of websites related to the subject of this book.
This site is updated regularly. Please use this link to access the list:
www.powerkidslinks.com/guide/arctic/

Index